Seven Days to Care for God's World

By Dean and Donna Erickson
Illustrated by Kathy Rogers

AUGSBURG ● **MINNEAPOLIS**

This book is printed on recycled paper that meets the 50% waste paper requirements established by the United States government for recycled paper products.

Library of Congress Cataloging-in-Publication Data

Erickson, Dean, 1949–
    Seven days to care for God's world / by Dean and Donna Erickson ; illustrated by Kathy Rogers.
       p.   cm.
    ISBN 0-8066-2533-3
    1. Creation—Juvenile literature. 2. Human ecology—Religious aspects—Juvenile literature. I. Erickson, Donna, 1949–
II. Title.
BS651.E76   1991
231.7'65—dc20
                                           91-8875
                                             CIP

Manufactured in the U.S.A.   AF 9-2533

95 94 93 92 91   2 3 4 5 6 7 8 9 10

This book is dedicated to our children,
Bjorn, Britt, and Anders Erickson,
who inspire us to take care of the earth
they will inherit,
and to
John Erik Anduri,
who encourages all of us
to celebrate God's creation.

This is Rupert. Rupert is seven years old. He likes playing soccer, riding his bike, and playing with his friends. But what he likes best is going to his grandparents' house every summer to help them take care of their big garden.

This year Rupert is staying at Grandma and Grandpa's house for a whole week. On the first morning of his stay, as he lay in bed half-awake, thinking about all the fun things he was going to do that day, he heard Grandpa calling, "Rupert, time to get up! Breakfast is on the table, and there's work to do in the garden."

That's what Rupert was waiting to hear. He was up in a flash, dressed, and at the table ready to eat.

Grandpa, Grandma, and Rupert held hands as Grandpa said grace. "Thank you, God, for the good food you have given us and for our grandson Rupert whom we love very much. Amen."

"Amen," said Rupert.

"You need to eat a big breakfast when you are going to work in the garden," said Grandpa. Rupert didn't need any encouragement—he loved Grandma's cooking!

After breakfast Rupert and Grandpa did the dishes. As they worked, Rupert told Grandpa all about his school and his friends and his soccer team. When the dishes were done, it was time to go outside. Rupert grabbed his hat from the hook by the door and ran down the path to the garden. The sights, sounds, and smells were all there, just as he remembered from last summer. Oh, how he loved the garden!

"Well, let's see," said Grandma, "we need to pull some weeds in the carrot patch, tie up some of the pea plants, water the flowers, and pick some beans. Let's get started."

The three gardeners worked hard all morning. The time flew by, and before Rupert knew it, Grandma had spread a blanket on the ground and had put out cookies and milk and coffee.

"All good gardeners need a break," said Grandma. "Who wants to help me eat some of these treats?"

"Working in the garden is fun, but eating in the garden is *really* fun," said Rupert, with a smile on his face and a cookie in his hand.

"Why does it feel so good to work in the garden?" he asked. "Even though it's hard work, I like it."

"It's because you are taking care of God's good earth," said Grandpa. "God created this earth, and just like this garden, God wants us to take care of it. When we are taking care of God's creation, we know we are doing what God wants, and that feels good."

"What about people who don't have gardens? How can they take care of God's creation?" asked Rupert.

"Taking care of God's creation means more than taking care of a garden like this," said Grandma. "I think of the whole world as a garden that needs our care."

"How do we do that?" asked Rupert. "I get tired just weeding *this* garden—how can I take care of the *whole world*?"

Grandpa smiled and gave Rupert a pat on the back. "You're right about that one, Rupert. We certainly can't take care of the whole world all by ourselves. For devotions this morning, let's read the creation story from the Bible. Maybe we can come up with some ways we can do our part to take care of this beautiful world God created."

"The first book of the Bible teaches us how God created the world in seven days," Grandma began.

" 'In the beginning God created the heavens and the earth. Now the earth was formless and empty, darkness was over the surface of the deep, and the Spirit of God was hovering over the waters. And God said, "Let there be light," and there was light. God saw that the light was good, and he separated the light from the darkness. God called the light "day" and the darkness he called "night." And there was evening, and there was morning—the first day.' "

"The first day of creation is about light," said Grandma. "Just think, none of these plants would grow without sunlight."

"The Bible talks a lot about light," added Grandpa. "Can you think of anything that has to do with light that would help us take better care of God's creation?" he asked.

"Well," said Rupert, "Mom and Dad always tell me to turn off the lights at home when I'm not using them. They say that it costs money to run the lights and we shouldn't waste energy. Maybe I could do a better job of turning off lights . . . but even though I know that God is always with me, can I still keep my night light on?"

"Sure, Rupert," Grandpa said with a smile. "It's good to remember to turn off lights when you're not using them. Besides saving energy, it helps cut down on air pollution."

"How?" Rupert asked.

"Well, some power plants burn coal or oil to make electricity. The burning can pollute the air," said Grandpa.

"Let's continue reading the creation story," said Grandma. "The next few verses talk about the second day: 'And God said, "Let there be an expanse between the waters to separate water from water." . . . And it was so. God called the expanse "sky." And there was evening, and there was morning—the second day.'

"God's garden includes the beautiful, blue sky," said Grandma. "Unfortunately, there are some places in this world where people have made the air so dirty, they can't see the beautiful sky anymore."

"I know that cars pollute the air with their exhaust," said Rupert. "One thing I can do to help take care of the sky is walk or ride my bicycle more and not always ask Mom or Dad to drive me places."

"Cars can be very useful," said Grandpa, "but we should all look for ways to use them less. We can plan our errands so we don't have to drive so much, or share a ride with someone, or ride the bus. Your idea of riding your bike is good."

"I like riding my bike," said Rupert. "If I can do things that are fun and still help take care of God's world, that's great!"

"The third day of creation was a busy one," said Grandma. "God created the land, the seas, and after that, all sorts of growing things. Listen to this: 'Then God said, "Let the land produce vegetation: seed-bearing plants and trees on the land that bear fruit with seed in it, according to their various kinds." And it was so. . . . And God saw it was good. And there was evening, and there was morning—the third day.' "

"Wow, what a day that must have been!" said Rupert. "All those beautiful flowers and plants and trees—what can I do to help take care of this part of creation?"

"Well, Rupert, remember last year when you helped me plant those new trees in front of the house?" asked Grandpa. "We were helping take care of God's world. Trees not only give us fruit and shade and a place to climb, but they help make our air cleaner, too."

"You're kidding!" said Rupert. "How?"

"Well," said Grandpa, "it may be hard to understand, but trees take something out of the air that we can't breathe—called carbon dioxide—and turn it into oxygen, something we *can* breathe. Trees are God's air cleaners, and it's very important to take care of them."

"Why do people cut down trees, if they are so important?" asked Rupert.

"For a number of reasons," explained Grandpa. "Trees are cut down to clear land for farms, factories, and places for people to live. Sometimes new trees are planted to replace the ones cut down, but not always."

"Like in the rain forests?" asked Rupert. "We talked about that in school."

"That's a good example of valuable trees being lost—along with the living creatures that make the rain forest their home," said Grandpa. "But closer to home, we are cutting down trees too. Some of the wood is used to build things—like houses and furniture—and some of it is used to make paper."

"Paper? I didn't know that!" exclaimed Rupert. "But I *do* know that a lot of paper gets thrown away. Mom says that's a big problem, because we're running out of places to put our garbage. She said some companies find ways to reuse old paper—you know, recycle it. We save our old newspapers for recycling, instead of throwing them out."

"Recycling is a good way to take care of God's earth," said Grandma. "And we can recycle more than paper. We can recycle glass and aluminum and other metals. Even some plastics are recyclable. The more we recycle and reuse, the less garbage we have!"

"What happened on the fourth day of creation, Grandma?" asked Rupert.

"Let's read about it," said Grandma. " 'God made two great lights—the greater light to govern the day and the lesser light to govern the night. He also made the stars. . . . And God saw that it was good. And there was evening, and there was morning—the fourth day.' "

"In school we studied the sun," said Rupert. "I learned about using energy from the sun—it's called solar energy. My teacher said solar energy doesn't cause pollution like other kinds of energy can."

"See the clothes drying on the line over there?" said Grand-pa. "That's one of the easiest ways to use solar energy. The sun and the wind dry our clothes."

"And make them smell nice too!" said Grandma.

"On the fifth day of creation God made the birds and fish," she continued. " 'And God said, "Let the water teem with living creatures, and let birds fly above the earth across the expanse of the sky." So God created the great creatures of the sea and every living and moving thing with which the water teems, according to their kinds, and every winged bird according to its kind. And God saw that it was good.' "

"How can I help take care of birds and fish?" asked Rupert. "Don't they take care of themselves?"

"Sure they take care of themselves," said Grandpa, "but we may be doing some things that hurt them and not even know it."

"Like what?" asked Rupert.

"We use fertilizer in our garden to help our plants grow. When it rains, some of the fertilizer washes into rivers and lakes where fish and birds live. We have to make sure that the fertilizer we use isn't dangerous for living things."

"Clean water is very precious," said Grandma.

"You're right!" agreed Rupert. "Dad told me that when I'm brushing my teeth I should only run the water when I start brushing and when I'm finished—not the whole time. He said our family could save many gallons of water each week just by doing that."

"We shouldn't waste water or any of God's gifts to us," said Grandma. Rupert and Grandpa nodded.

"We have two more days of creation left to go," said Grandma.

"I don't think we've read about *people* being created yet," said Rupert. "Aren't we part of God's world too?"

"We sure are," said Grandma. "Listen to what was created on the sixth day: ' "Let the land produce living creatures according to their kinds: livestock, creatures that move along the ground, and wild animals, each according to its kind." And it was so. . . . And God saw that it was good. Then God said, "Let us make man in our image, in our likeness, and let them rule over the fish of the sea and the birds of the air, over the livestock, over all the earth, and over all the creatures that move along the ground." So God created man in his own image, in the image of God he created him; male and female he created them.' "

"So we need to take care of people too," said Rupert.

"Sometimes it's easy to forget that people need our care," said Grandma. "When we sit in our beautiful garden and look at everything around us, we should also think about ways to help others."

"Our church collects food to give to people who are hungry," said Rupert.

"Being kind and generous to others is a good way to help them," suggested Grandpa. "Grandma and I use some of the things we grow right here in our garden to help people. We bring flowers from our garden to cheer up people in the hospital, and we share our garden's vegetables with our neighbors."

"It seems like everything has been created, but we've only talked about six days. Aren't there seven days in the week?" asked Rupert. "What happened on the last day?"

"The seventh day is as important as any of the other days of creation," said Grandma, picking up her Bible. " 'By the seventh day God had finished the work he had been doing; so on the seventh day he rested from all his work. And God blessed the seventh day and made it holy, because on it he rested from all the work of creating that he had done.' "

"God rested on the seventh day," said Grandpa, "and so should we. God commanded us to 'Remember the Sabbath day by keeping it holy.' One day out of our week is for rest and worship."

"And *every* day we should thank God for this beautiful creation!" added Grandma.

"Talking about rest makes me feel sleepy," yawned Rupert.

"I think we should all take a little rest before we go back to work," said Grandpa.

Rupert settled back in the thick, green grass. Yes, this was his favorite place in all God's creation. *Thank you, God, for making such a beautiful world,* Rupert thought, as his eyes began to close. *I promise to do all I can to take care of it!*

When Rupert returned home from his grandparents' house, he thought it would be fun to start a special project with his family. He called it "We Care about God's World!" Would you like to start the same project with your family? Here's how!

WE CARE ABOUT GOD'S WORLD!

Rupert's family got off to a good start by choosing a theme verse and a theme song. Everybody learned the Bible verse and the song to remind them of why we need to take care of God's good creation. Here's what they chose—maybe you and your family would like to use it too.

Theme Scripture Verse: "The earth is the Lord's, and everything in it, the world, and all who live in it" (Psalm 24:1).

Theme Song: "All Things Bright and Beautiful"

Mrs. Cecil F. Alexander   Old English Melody

Refrain

All things bright and beau - ti - ful, all crea - tures great and small,

all things wise and won - der - ful, the Lord God made them all.

1. Each lit - tle flow'r that o - pens, each lit - tle bird that sings,
2. The pur - ple head - ed moun - tain, the riv - er run - ning by,

he made their glow - ing col - ors, he made their ti - ny wings.
the sun - set, and the morn - ing that bright - ens up the sky.

"We Care about God's World!" Progress Chart

Now that you have a theme verse and song, you have some planning to do. Just how *does* your family care for God's world? You might want to make a chart to remind your family of ways you can help care for creation. You'll need the following supplies:

- large piece of paper or poster board (You might use the back of an old poster.)
- marking pens or crayons
- used postage stamps (especially nature pictures) or stickers (Check advertising mail that comes to your house—often letters contain free stickers or stamps.)

Once you have gathered the necessary supplies, hold a family meeting to discuss the things you can do to help take care of the earth. List all your ideas, making sure to include things that even the youngest member of your family can do. After you have made your list, draw a grid on your poster as shown. Across the top, write the activities your family will try to do to help care for the earth. Down the left side, write the names of everyone in your family.

Each time someone remembers to do one of the activities you have listed, that person can record it in the appropriate space with one of your recycled stamps or stickers or by simply drawing a picture in the spot.

Rupert's family decided they should have some rewards from time to time for remembering to do things that helped creation. Every time seven spots were covered, they went out for ice cream or pizza, or they went roller skating or biking together. You might want to think of some other rewards (besides the good feeling you get caring for God's world)!

Activity	pick up litter	sort out papers	crush cans	compost	cardboard	collect plastic	
Mom	❀		♥				
Dad	🧸	♥		❀	☺		
Rupert	🧸		☺				

Every good project needs a logo! Here's what Rupert designed. His family used it to make T-shirts for the whole family. You can do the same thing—here's how!

You will need: plain T-shirt for each person (100% cotton works best)
fabric paint in squeeze bottles (variety of colors)
carbon transfer paper (available at fabric and craft stores)
waxed paper or cardboard

Place a piece of waxed paper or cardboard between the two layers of the shirt to protect the backside from any paint that might soak through. Place the carbon paper on top of the shirt, carbon side down, and the logo from this book (or a photocopy of it) on top of the carbon paper. Lightly trace around the logo, being careful not to move the paper or the shirt. Once the logo is transferred to the shirt, squeeze out paint along the carbon lines (the lines will wash out). Allow each color to dry before proceeding to the next. Let everyone paint his or her own shirt. (Adapted from *Prime Time Together . . . with Kids* by Donna Erickson, copyright © 1989 Augsburg Fortress.)

One of the things Rupert learned was the importance of recycling. Here are some recycling ideas for your family to try:

Turn an old milk carton into a bird feeder

You will need: 1 clean, empty half-gallon milk carton
2 wooden or metal skewers or thin wooden dowels, 8" long
scissor
wire or string
food items for birds

Cut out two 3" circles opposite each other, 2" from the bottom of the carton. Poke one skewer through the carton directly below the circles to make a perch for the birds. (If you are using a dowel, sharpen one end with a pencil sharpener.) Poke the second skewer diagonally through one uncut side of the carton, about 6" up from the bottom of the carton. Put food onto the skewer through one of the holes in the side of the carton, and then poke the skewer back outside the carton about 2" from the bottom of the other uncut side (see illustration). Attach a piece of wire or string to the top of the carton and hang the feeder in a tree in your yard.

Try these foods to attract some feathered friends, and check with a local bird expert for other ideas:
Orange pieces for orioles
Apple slices in the early spring for finches
Watermelon slices for hummingbirds
Dried bread, dinner rolls, bagels, suet, or seed balls for a variety of birds

Shape up old crayons

You will need: old color crayons (the broken ones!)
several small empty glass jars, one for each color
roaster rack
medium-size, shallow saucepan
plastic candy mold tray in shapes children like (available at kitchen supply stores)

Don't throw away all those broken crayons! You don't have to go out and buy new ones, you can "shape up" the old! Start by removing the paper wrappers from each crayon. Then, under adult supervision, break the crayons into small pieces and put them into glass jars, separating colors. Place the jars on the roasting rack in a saucepan filled with enough water to cover ½" of the jars. Heat the water until the crayons melt.

Let your adult supervisor carefully pour the melted wax into the plastic candy mold tray. The wax will harden quickly and pop out of the mold easily. For added effect, pour a contrasting color in the mold after the first layer of wax has hardened. This will produce a two-tone crayon.

Recycled crayons make great party favors. And for fun, you can use them as a puzzle—just let preschoolers put the different shapes back into the candy mold!

Use the sun to bake a snack

You will need: 1 large piece of black construction paper
aluminum foil
glue
paper clips
1 small, clear glass cup or dish
plastic wrap
apple slices, raisins

To make the oven, cut out paper and foil as illustrated. Glue the foil, shiny side up, to the paper. When the glue has dried, roll the paper/foil into a cone shape, attaching ends together with paper clips.

To cook your snack, place the apple slices and raisins in the glass dish and cover it with plastic wrap. Place the oven outside with cone opening toward the sun. Carefully set the glass dish inside the oven at the base of the cone. To maintain maximum heat in the oven, keep it toward the sun at all times as the apples cook. Check the apples after 15-20 minutes to see if they are baked. For best results, use your oven on a hot, sunny day. Enjoy your treat—don't burn yourself!